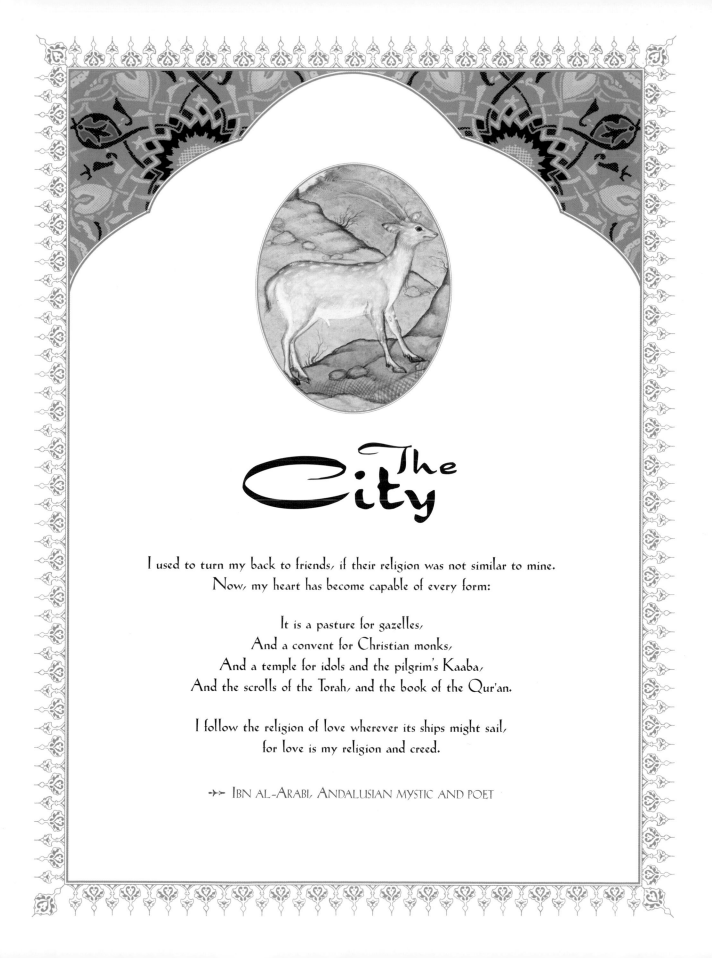

The City

I used to turn my back to friends, if their religion was not similar to mine.
Now, my heart has become capable of every form:

It is a pasture for gazelles,
And a convent for Christian monks,
And a temple for idols and the pilgrim's Kaaba,
And the scrolls of the Torah, and the book of the Qur'an.

I follow the religion of love wherever its ships might sail,
for love is my religion and creed.

↠ IBN AL-ARABI, ANDALUSIAN MYSTIC AND POET

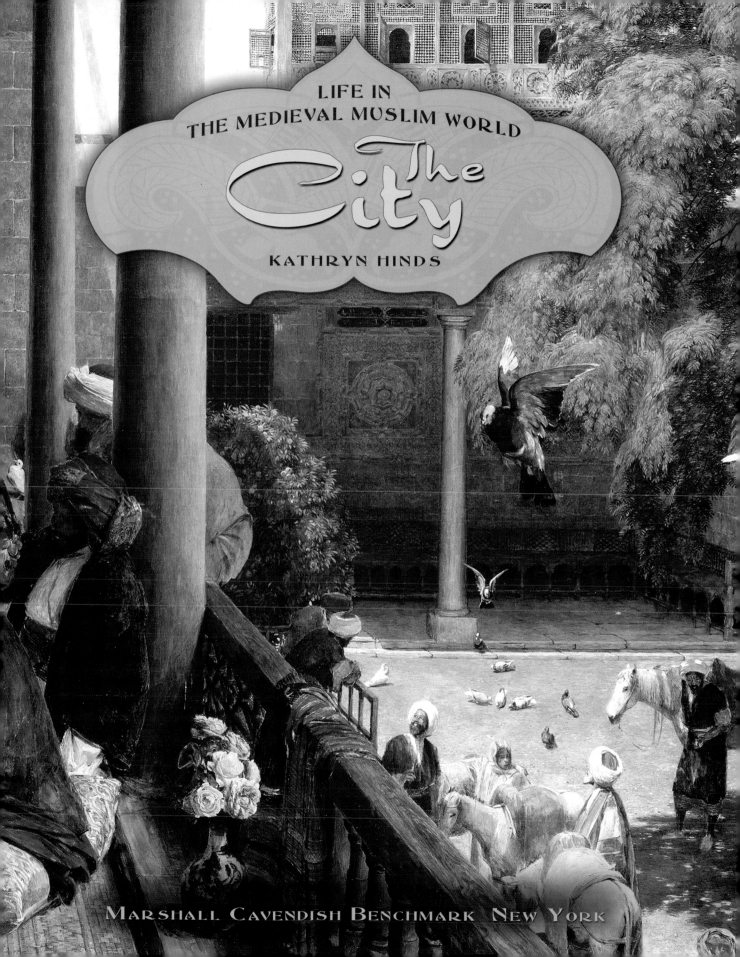

LIFE IN
THE MEDIEVAL MUSLIM WORLD

The City

KATHRYN HINDS

MARSHALL CAVENDISH BENCHMARK NEW YORK

To Fox

The author and publishers wish to extend heartfelt thanks to Dr. Josef W. Meri, Fellow and Special Scholar in Residence, Royal Aal al-Bayt Institute for Islamic Thought, Amman, Jordan, for his gracious and invaluable assistance in reviewing the manuscript of this book.

MARSHALL CAVENDISH BENCHMARK 99 WHITE PLAINS ROAD TARRYTOWN, NEW YORK 10591 www.marshallcavendish.us Text copyright © 2009 by Marshall Cavendish Corporation. Map copyright © 2009 by Mike Reagan. All rights reserved. No part of this book may be reproduced or utilized in any form or by any means electronic or mechanical including photocopying, recording, or by any information storage and retrieval system, without permission from the copyright holders. All Internet sites were available and accurate when this book was sent to press. LIBRARY OF CONGRESS CATALOGING-IN-PUBLICATION DATA Hinds, Kathryn, 1962- The city / by Kathryn Hinds. p. cm. — (Life in the medieval Muslim world) Includes bibliographical references and index. Summary: "A social history of the Islamic world from the eighth through the mid-thirteenth century, with a focus on life in the cities"—Provided by publisher. ISBN 978-0-7614-3089-6 1. Islamic countries—Juvenile literature. 2. Islamic countries—Social life and customs—Juvenile literature. 3. Islamic cities and towns—Juvenile literature. I. Title. DS36.6.H56 2008 909'.0976701—dc22 2008019432

EDITOR: Joyce Needleman Stanton   PUBLISHER: Michelle Bisson
ART DIRECTOR: Anahid Hamparian   SERIES DESIGNER: Kristen Branch / Michael Nelson Design

Printed in China
135642

front cover: Inside an old house in nineteenth-century Cairo, decorated much as medieval homes were
half-title page: A gazelle pictured in a manuscript from Muslim-ruled northern India
title page: Men enjoy their midday meal in Old Cairo in this 1875 painting by John Frederick Lewis.
back cover: Birds perched in a palm tree, painted by Abdullah ibn al-Fadl in 1222

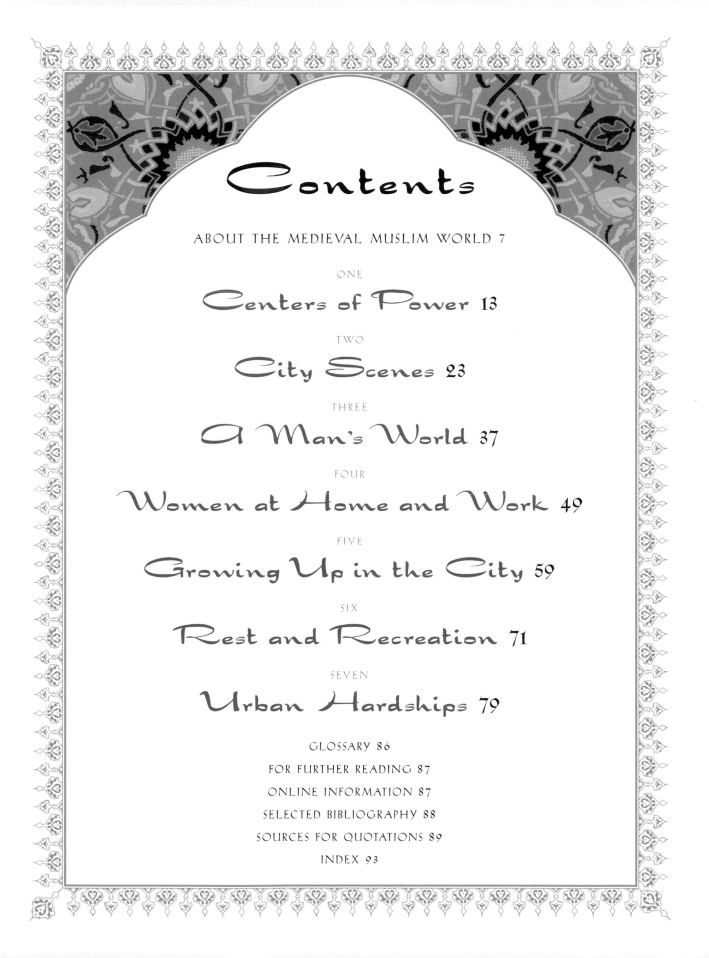

Contents

Muhammad left the
city of Mecca, where
he was unwelcome,
and journeyed across
the desert to make a
new home in Medina.

About the
Medieval Muslim World

IN THE YEAR 622 AN ARABIAN MERCHANT NAMED Muhammad, accompanied by two hundred followers, left his home city of Mecca for the troubled town of Yathrib. Its citizens knew that Muhammad had been receiving visions from God and preaching what God had revealed to him. His message was unpopular in Mecca, but the people of Yathrib welcomed Muhammad to be their chief judge and embraced his teaching of Islam, or submission to God. They recognized Muhammad as the Prophet of God, and their city soon became known as Madinat al-Nabi, "City of the Prophet," or simply Medina.

The Hegira, Muhammad's move to Medina, marked the beginning of the Islamic community, the *umma*. From that point on, the community of Muslims (followers of Islam) grew rapidly. By 634 it embraced the entire Arabian Peninsula. By 750 Muslim rulers controlled a wide band of territory from the Iberian Peninsula, across North Africa, to the borders of India. During the following centuries the *umma* continued to expand into India, Anatolia (modern Turkey), Central Asia, and sub-Saharan Africa. Along the way, Arab and local cultures mingled and sometimes melded, leading to the

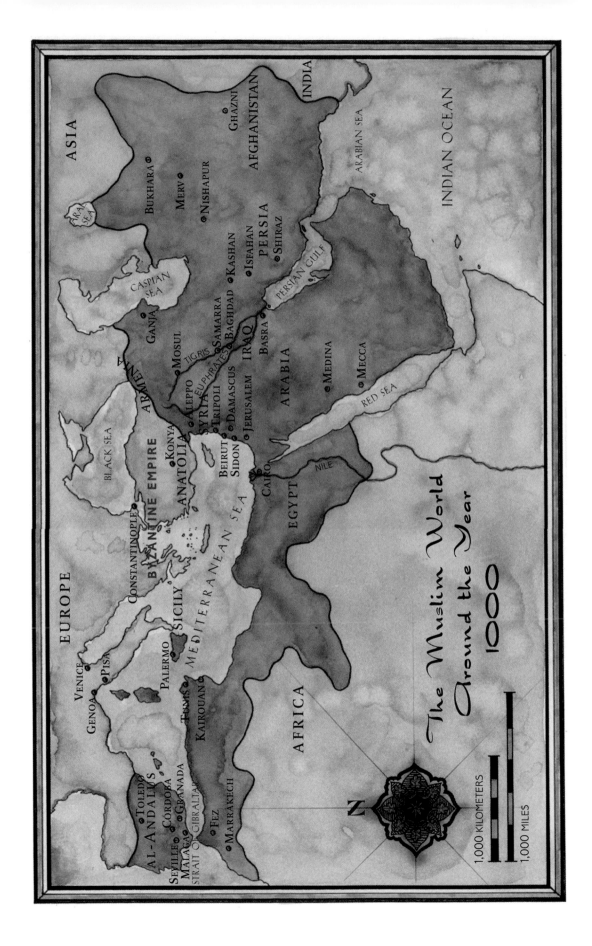

The Muslim World Around the Year 1000

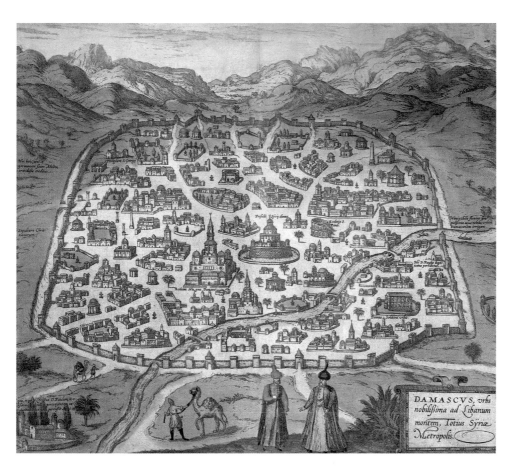

Damascus, Syria, was one of the great cities of the medieval Muslim world.

development of a shared Muslim culture with many ways of expressing itself.

The Dar al-Islam, "Abode of Islam," was politically united for only a brief period. But it remained united in other important ways, through religious beliefs and language. Arabic, the language of the Qur'an (the holy book of Islam), became the common tongue of nearly all Muslims in Islam's early centuries. In most areas it was used not just in religion but also in government, law, literature, and learning. This meant that no matter where a Muslim went in the Dar al-Islam, he or she would be able to share news and knowledge with other Muslims. In fact the gathering, communication, and spreading of knowledge and skills in the arts and sciences was one of the great achievements of the Muslim world during this era. For this reason, it is often referred to as the Golden Age of Islam. In the history of the West, this time is generally called the Middle Ages, and for convenience we use both that term and *medieval* for this period even when discussing areas outside Europe.

The Dar al-Islam and Christian medieval Europe often conflicted with each other. Yet there was also a great deal of peaceful interchange between the two, in many ways to the lasting benefit of European civilization. And at various times and places in the medieval Muslim world, Muslims, Christians, and Jews lived and worked side by side in an atmosphere of tolerance seldom found elsewhere in the past. In the present, too, we can find much to learn from both the successes and the struggles of the Dar al-Islam in the Middle Ages.

This series of books looks at the lives of the people who lived in that diverse world, focusing mainly on the Middle East and Spain in the eighth through thirteenth centuries. In this volume we will meet the people of the medieval Muslim world's cities: merchants and craftspeople, students and scholars, housewives and workers. We will visit their homes and markets and schools, and discover the sights, sounds, and smells that surrounded city people. We will see what kinds of work they did, how they relaxed, and how they coped with life's hardships. So step back into history, to a time of faith and intellect, intrigue and excitement, struggle and splendor. Welcome to life in the medieval Muslim world!

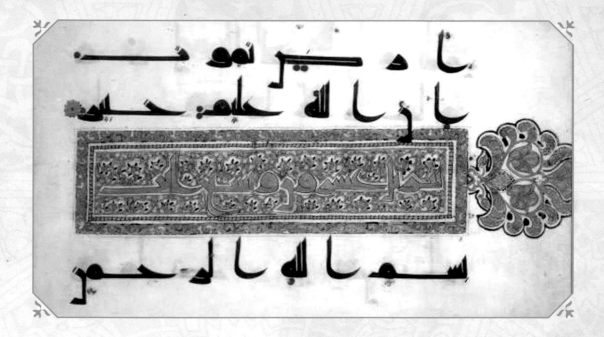

A Note on Dates and Names

For Muslims the Hegira (Arabic *hijra*, "departure" or "emigration") began a new age and so became the year 1 of the Muslim calendar. Dates in this calendar are labeled AH, for *Anno Hegira*, or simply H. For ease of reading, though, this series of books uses the conventional Western dating system. Also for ease of reading, we are using the common Westernized forms of many Arabic names—for example, *Avicenna* instead of *Ibn Sina*—and we are leaving out most of the special accent marks that scholars use when converting Arabic names to the Western alphabet. There are many different ways to convert Arabic to English, especially because the Arabic alphabet does not include symbols for most vowels. For this reason, you may see the same names spelled in slightly different ways in different books. In many sources you may also see the God of Islam referred to as Allah. Since the Arabic word *Allah* simply means *God* and refers to the same deity worshipped by Jews and Christians, we have chosen to use *God* instead of *Allah* in this series.

Above: This chapter heading from a ninth-century Qur'an uses elegantly stylized lettering.

The Great Mosque
of Mecca, pictured
in the nineteenth
century by a Muslim
artist. In the center
of the courtyard is
the Kaaba.

ONE

Centers of Power

These centers were the pillars of the country.

→ AL-RUNDI, THIRTEENTH-CENTURY ANDALUSIAN POET

ROM THE BEGINNING, CITIES PLAYED A commanding role in the spread, development, and maintenance of Muslim culture. Islam was founded in Mecca, a city that had become prosperous due to its position on a main trade route taken by caravans. Mecca was also home to the Kaaba, a major religious shrine, which people from all parts of Arabia visited long before the coming of Islam. Even warring tribes observed a truce when they came to the city to visit this special place. During such times the Meccans held fairs that brought the people of Arabia together to trade as well as worship. When Mecca became a Muslim city, the pilgrimages and fairs continued, with the Kaaba now dedicated to God alone rather than to the many deities honored by the pre-Islamic Arabians.

13

Being both the location of the Kaaba and the Prophet Muhammad's birthplace, Mecca was the holiest city in Islam. Second to it was Medina, where the *umma* was first established and took root. Roughly two hundred miles north of Mecca, Medina was an oasis town. When Muhammad arrived there, its citizens made their living largely from farming. Like the Meccans, the people of Medina belonged to many different clans and tribes, or extended family groups. Unlike the Meccans, the Medinans were suffering through a violent feud between the town's two major tribes. Muhammad settled the feud, brought peace to Medina, and united all the people of the area under the banner of Islam.

His role as peacemaker and uniter made Muhammad Medina's political as well as spiritual leader. "Whatever you may disagree about shall be referred to God and Muhammad," instructed the Constitution of Medina, a document drawn up after he brought the clans together. In it he also declared the Medinans "a community to the exclusion of other people." This was the beginning of the Muslim state, whose influence and power spread throughout the Arabian Peninsula in the years leading up to Muhammad's death in 632. The capital of this new political and religious community was naturally Medina, and it remained so during the reign of the first four caliphs, "successors," who followed Muhammad as leaders of the *umma*.

DAMASCUS AND BAGHDAD

By 656 Arab Muslim armies had conquered Syria and Egypt from the Greek Byzantine Empire, and Iraq from the Persian Sasanian Empire. Soldiers who settled in these new provinces lived in camps and garrisons, many of which eventually developed into cities—an example is Basra in Iraq. One function of the garrisons was to collect

JERUSALEM

After Mecca and Medina, the third holiest city in the Islamic world was (and is) Jerusalem. Here one of the earliest Muslim monuments, the Dome of the Rock, was built over the spot where, in a vision, Muhammad had made a mystical journey to heaven. The city was a thriving commercial center in the region known to medieval people as Syria. Much of Jerusalem's prosperity was due to the fact that it was also sacred to Jews and Christians, who came to the city in great numbers to visit its holy places. For Jews, Jerusalem was especially significant as the site of the Temple, the heart of their ancient homeland.

At some periods people of the three faiths were able to peacefully coexist in the holy city—but at other times it was a focus of bitter conflict. The Jewish philosopher and poet Yehuda Halevi lived during the time that Jerusalem was held by Christian Crusaders (known in the Muslim world as Franks). Although he had a comfortable life in Córdoba, he longed to go to the Holy Land more than anything:

> My heart is in the East, and I am at the end of the West—
> How can I taste what I eat, how can it be sweet to me?
> How can I fulfil my vow of pilgrimage, while yet
> [Jerusalem] is in Frankish bonds, and I am in Arab chains.
> I hold it light to leave all the bounty of Spain,
> as I hold it dear to see the dust of the ruined sanctuary.

Eventually Halevi did follow his dream and leave al-Andalus for "the East," where he lived out the rest of his life.

Above: Jerusalem, revered by all the peoples of Abraham—Jews, Christians, and Muslims—sparkles in a golden light in this mosaic from a church in Italy.

taxes from the conquered peoples. As a result, military and financial resources were now concentrated in areas far from Medina.

In 661 Mu'awiya, governor of the province of Syria, became the first caliph of the Umayyad dynasty of rulers. Rather than move to Medina, he remained in his provincial headquarters, the ancient city of Damascus. For almost a hundred years, it was the capital city of the Dar al-Islam. Even after that, it remained a leading center of trade and culture, renowned for its Great Mosque, its markets, the fertility of its surrounding countryside, and the fine silks, swords, and armor produced by its craftspeople. Ibn Jubayr, a twelfth-century visitor from Granada (in southern Spain), was particularly struck by the beauties of Damascus:

> She is the paradise of the Orient, the place where dawned her gracious and radiant beauty, the seal of the lands of Islam where we have sought hospitality, and the bride of the cities we have observed. She is garnished with the flowers of sweet-scented herbs, and bedecked in the brocaded vestments of gardens. In the place of beauty she holds a sure position. . . . If Paradise is on earth then Damascus without a doubt is in it.

The Umayyads were followed by the Abbasid dynasty, which came to power largely with the help of Persian military support. By this time Muslim rule extended through Persia and into what are now Uzbekistan and Afghanistan, and the caliphs wanted to be closer to these eastern parts of their domain. So the second Abbasid caliph, al-Mansur, moved the capital from Damascus to Baghdad, Iraq, beside the Tigris River where it flows close to the Euphrates. Al-Mansur considered several factors when choosing this site:

It is best to settle here, midway between these four agricultural districts. . . . Thus you will have palm plantations on every side of you and water near at hand: if harvest fails or is late from one district, you can get relief from another. You can get provisions by the Sarat canal from the Euphrates river traffic. Egyptian and Syrian caravans will come here by the desert roads, and all kinds of China goods upriver from the sea, and Byzantine and Mosul produce down the Tigris. With rivers on both sides, no enemy can approach except by ship or bridge.

Damascus was a hub of culture and commerce throughout the medieval period. The Great Mosque, with its many arches and large courtyard, is at the center of this illustration.

The building of Baghdad was a massive project involving tens of thousands of workmen. Laborers came from all over the region to join the construction crews, which were paid a good, reliable daily wage. There was already a small village on the site, but the caliph wanted a brand-new, carefully planned city. It was perfectly round, surrounded by a high mud-brick wall with gates in the northeast, southeast, southwest, and northwest. At the very center of the

Baghdad's location along the Tigris assured an ample water supply, and the river also gave traveling merchants easy access to the splendid city. These advantages outweighed the risk of occasional floods.

Round City were the main mosque and the palace. The area around them was probably intended for markets but came to be filled with government offices, barracks for soldiers, and other official buildings. Markets, shops, workshops, the homes of ordinary citizens, the mansions of the rich, and the palaces of high officials were all located outside the Round City's wall. Eventually a number of royal palaces were also built outside the wall, on the banks of the Tigris.

At the Abbasids' height of prestige and power, in the eighth and ninth centuries, Baghdad was *the* place to be in the Middle East. It was home to many of the wealthiest, most talented, most intelligent, most skillful people in the Islamic world. Poets, musicians, artists, and scholars all gathered in the capital. Merchants and travelers from as far away as Scandinavia and China came to trade and to see the wonders of this great city. Baghdad's population itself was extremely diverse, as was true of most medieval Muslim cities, with Christians and Jews living alongside Muslims, while Arabs, Turks, Persians, and Indians mingled with one another in the markets and other public places.

THE CITIES OF AL-ANDALUS

In 711 a Muslim army from North Africa crossed the Strait of Gibraltar* and conquered most of the Iberian Peninsula. In 756

Gibraltar comes from the Arabic name for the Rock of Gibraltar, *Jabal Tariq*—"the mountain of Tariq," referring to the leader of the conquest, Tariq ibn Ziyad. Many other Spanish place names and words are also derived from Arabic.

The City

Muslim Spain—or al-Andalus, as it was known in Arabic—came under the control of the Umayyad dynasty, which reigned there for several generations, even when the rest of the Muslim world was under Abbasid rule. The capital of al-Andalus was the city of Córdoba, which became the largest and most splendid city in western Europe. A tenth-century author wrote that Córdoba and its suburbs contained just over 213,000 houses:

> This figure includes the dwellings of the common people such as workmen and artisans, but excludes the rented attics, inns, baths and taverns. The palaces of the nobles, viziers, officials of the royal household, generals and wealthy citizens, the barracks, hospitals, colleges and other public buildings come to a total of 60,300.

Córdoba had wide paved streets, running water, thriving crafts industries and marketplaces, and notable centers of learning. There were seventy libraries. Most of them were private, but scholars could easily make arrangements to use them. The library of the caliph, said to contain around 400,000 books, was especially famous. As one Córdoban Christian remarked, under Muslim rule his city was "elevated with honors, expanded in glory, piled full of riches, and with great energy filled with an abundance of all the delights of the world, more than one can believe or express."

Umayyad rule in al-Andalus lasted until 1031, when new waves of conquerors began to arrive from North Africa. At the same time, the Christian kingdoms of northern Spain were gradually overcoming the Muslim cities. Al-Andalus broke up into a number of city-states, such as Toledo, Seville, and Granada. Many of these became great centers of learning and culture in their own right.

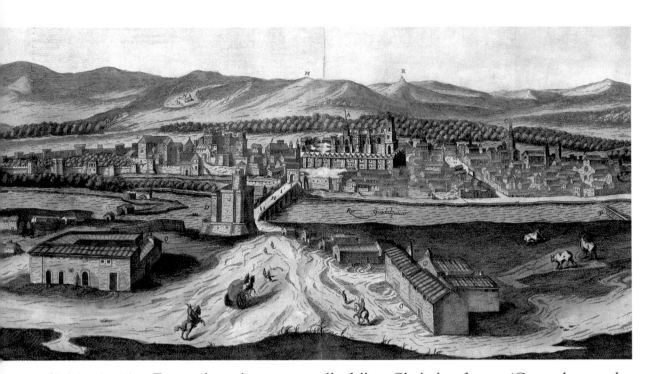

Córdoba, along the Guadalquivir River, was one of the most refined—and cleanest—cities in western Europe.

Even when they eventually fell to Christian forces (Granada was the last to do so, in 1492), they passed on their intellectual and artistic legacies, which remain part of the fabric of Spain today.

CAIRO

In 641 the Arab Muslim conquerors of Egypt established a military base just south of the Nile Delta, and this garrison grew into the city of Fustat. It soon became Egypt's leading city, an important center of trade with control over the caravan routes to both east and west. The geographer al-Muqaddasi visited Fustat in the second half of the tenth century and found it delightful in every way:

> It has superceded Baghdad, and is the glory of Islam, and is the marketplace for all mankind. . . . Victuals here are most appetizing, their savories superb. Confectionaries are cheap, bananas plentiful, as are fresh dates; vegetables and firewood

are abundant. The water is palatable, the air salubrious. It is a treasury of learned men; and the winter here is agreeable.

Even as the geographer was praising Fustat, however, right next to it a new city was gaining prominence. Cairo, founded in 969 by the Fatimid dynasty of North African rulers, soon surpassed its neighbor in size and splendor. Eventually the "sister cities" merged, with Fustat coming to be known as Old Cairo.

The heart of Cairo was the al-Azhar Mosque, which was not only a house of worship but also the home of one of the Muslim world's greatest centers of learning. This academy is regarded as the world's first university, and it set the pattern for many aspects of higher education, such as a distinction between undergraduate and graduate studies. Another institution that contributed to Cairo's reputation as an intellectual haven was the House of Knowledge, founded by the caliph in 1005. This was a library that contained "manuscripts in all the domains of science and culture, to an extent to which they had never been brought together for a prince." The House of Knowledge was open to anyone who wanted to read its books. People could also make copies to take home, and the caliph himself donated paper, ink, and pens for this purpose.

Old Cairo kept much of its medieval character well into the modern era.

Scholars flocked to Cairo, and so did scientists, philosophers, writers, architects, artists, merchants, administrators, soldiers, and ordinary workers. They were all drawn by the city's power, prosperity, and opportunities. In the 1300s the Tunisian historian Ibn Khaldun praised Cairo as "the mother of the world, the great center of Islam, and the mainspring of the sciences and the crafts." Today it remains one of the great capitals of Islamic culture.

Centers of Power

21

TWO

City Scenes

Córdoba is made up of five continuous cities, each surrounded by walls that divide it from the rest, and possessing enough markets, hostelries, baths and buildings for the different professions.
↣ AL-IDRISI, TWELFTH-CENTURY NORTH AFRICAN GEOGRAPHER

ALONGSIDE THE GREAT CAPITALS OF THE medieval Muslim world were numerous thriving provincial cities. Among them were Fez, Tunis, and Kairouan in North Africa; Palermo in Sicily; Aleppo, Tripoli, and Jerusalem in Syria; Konya in Anatolia; Shiraz, Isfahan, and Nishapur in Persia; Ghazni in Afghanistan; and Merv and Bukhara in Central Asia. These cities differed according to their climates and resources—for example, many parts of the Dar al-Islam had little wood available, so most of the buildings would be constructed of brick or stone. There were also some cultural differences, particularly in Persia, where the Persian language never completely gave way to Arabic. In fact,

Opposite: A provincial city in Anatolia, depicted in a Persian miniature painting from the 1500s. Mosques and schools cluster in the upper area, and trees and fountains beautify the surroundings.

Persian became a second language, especially for poetry, in much of the eastern part of the Muslim world. Despite such variations, though, cities across the Dar al-Islam had much in common.

GATHERING PLACES

In 836 the Abbasid capital was temporarily moved from Baghdad to Samarra, Iraq. This was another city that was precisely planned by the caliph:

> Al-Mutasim had architects brought and told them to choose the most suitable positions, and they selected a number of sites for the palaces. He gave each of his followers a palace to build. . . . Then he had plots of ground marked out for the military and civil officers and for the people, and likewise the Great Mosque. And he had the markets drawn out round the mosque with wide market rows, all the various kinds of merchandise being separate . . . according to the arrangement after which the markets of Baghdad were designed.

This description by a ninth-century historian shows what people considered to be the important ingredients in a city—and it is notable that primary among them are both the mosque and the markets. These two elements were so essential to urban life that they were literally at the center of almost every town or neighborhood.

The Mosque

"City mosques are of two kinds," the historian Ibn Khaldun explained, "great spacious ones which are prepared for holiday prayers, and other minor ones which are restricted to one section of the population or one quarter of the city and which are not for generally attended

prayers." The "great spacious" mosques were often called Friday Mosques, because they were where all of the city's Muslim men were expected to gather at noon every Friday to pray and listen to a sermon. The "minor ones," on the other hand, were local prayer halls where no sermons were preached; they could be visited at any time.

Originally each city had one Friday Mosque, but if the population grew too large for all the men to meet in a single location, additional great mosques were built. Their construction was usually ordered and funded by the ruler, as al-Muqaddasi relates of the Great Mosque of Damascus:

The Citadel of Cairo was a fortress begun by the chivalrous sultan Saladin around 1183. Over the following centuries it grew to a huge complex that included palaces, military barracks, government buildings, and mosques.

> The caliph al-Walid beheld Syria to be a country that had long been occupied by Christians and he noted there the beautiful churches still belonging to them, so enchantingly fair and so renowned for their splendour. . . . So he sought to build for the Muslims a mosque in Damascus that should be unique and a wonder to the world.

City Scenes

One of the many beautiful mosaics that adorn the Great Mosque of Damascus. With its lush plant life and flowing water, this image may have been intended to depict a dwelling in Paradise.

Al-Walid spared no expense in building the Damascus mosque. Thousands of craftsmen—including Persians, Indians, Egyptian Christians, and particularly Greeks—labored for ten years. When they were finished, the result was a building that many medieval Muslim writers described as the fourth wonder of the world. Counting as the fifth wonder was the building's beautiful decorations, especially the mosaics and marble carvings. It was said that a man could worship at the Great Mosque of Damascus every day of his adult life, and every day his eyes would light on some new marvel.

In the Middle Ages, the mosque was a multipurpose building. It was not only a place of prayer but, as we have already seen, could also be an educational center and gathering place for scholars. Law courts were held in the mosque, and city officials met in council there. It was the place where government decrees were read out and where people swore oaths of allegiance and alliance. It could function as a treasury for the safeguarding of the community's valuables, and had places for homeless people to sleep. Authors published their books by having them read aloud in the mosque. Merchants might even meet and do business there, and the city's commercial center was usually right next door.

The Marketplace

The market—known as the souk (Arabic *suq*) or bazaar (Persian *bazar*)—was vital to the city. In fact, according to vizier (chief administrator) Nizam al-Mulk, it was "one of the foundations of the state and is itself the product of justice." A thriving market meant a prosperous

Friends and business associates often met in the spacious corridors and courtyards of large urban mosques.

city, and prosperous cities meant prosperous states—especially since rulers received a variety of financial advantages from trade, such as customs duties and tolls collected from merchants.

It was not only rulers who benefited, of course. City dwellers could not survive without trade. The market was where a city's artists and craftspeople sold their wares, and where farmers from the surrounding countryside brought produce, livestock, firewood, and other necessities to sell to the urban population. (Some food could also be grown in orchards and gardens inside the city.)

For everyday needs, people usually went to a small neighborhood market. Cities also had large marketplaces that attracted shoppers and traders from other parts of the Dar al-Islam, and beyond. Eleventh-century Persian traveler Nasr-i Khusraw wrote this awed description of one of Cairo's markets:

> On the north side of the mosque is a bazaar called Suq al-Qanadil [Lamp Market], and no one ever saw such a bazaar anywhere else. Every sort of rare goods from all over the world can be had there: I saw tortoise-shell implements such as small boxes, combs, knife handles, and so on. I also saw extremely fine crystal, which the master craftsmen etch beautifully. . . . I saw elephant tusks from Zanzibar. . . . There was a type of skin from Abyssinia [Ethiopia] that resembled a leopard, from which they make sandals. Also from Abyssinia was a domesticated bird, large with white spots and a crown like a peacock's.

A marketplace in the medieval Muslim world was a network of streets lined with shops and stalls; often the entire complex was covered with a domed roof to give protection from the summer sun and winter rains. Craftsmen and tradesmen who dealt in the same type of goods clustered together in the same street or quarter—so there would be a shoemakers' street, a metalworkers' street, a booksellers' street, and so on. The most valuable goods were sold in a special area, usually at the market's center, that could be locked up at night.

Different cities and regions were known for specific products. Córdoba and Fez, for instance, were especially renowned for leather goods. Al-Muqaddasi wrote that Basra was famous for its exports of pearls and gems, henna, rosewater, medicinal minerals, linen and

silk fabrics, twenty-four types of fish, and forty-nine varieties of dates. He also detailed the products of many Syrian cities: "From Damascus come all these: olive-oil fresh-pressed, . . . brocade, oil of violets . . . , brass vessels, paper, nuts, dried figs and raisins." Of his hometown, he said: "From Jerusalem come cheeses, cotton, . . . raisins. . . , excellent apples, bananas . . .also pine-nuts . . . , and their equal is not found elsewhere; further mirrors, lamp-jars, and needles." Many cities produced distinctive textiles—different kinds of cloth woven from cotton, wool, silk, or linen—to sell both at home and abroad.

It was for specialties like these that importers and exporters traded and traveled. For example, an Andalusian civil servant wrote of Córdoba, "Merchants come from the ends of the earth, and traders from all the countries and far away islands stream into it. . . . They

Cairo's Khan el-Khalili bazaar was founded in the 1300s and has been home to shops selling a wide variety of goods ever since. This scene, painted in 1866, shows a rug market in the Khan.

City Scenes

29

bring spice and precious stone and royal merchandise and noble trade and all the precious goods of Egypt." Favorite items for long-distance trade were textiles, dyes (such as indigo), paper, medicines, and spices, all of which were fairly easy to transport and were also quite valuable.

Goods were carried by ship or caravan. The vessels that visited Cairo and the coastal cities of Syria came from many parts of the Dar al-Islam and also from such Mediterranean merchant powers as Venice, Pisa, Genoa, and Constantinople. In addition to the Mediterranean Sea, ships from Muslim countries plied the Red Sea and even the turbulent waters of the Indian Ocean. The Nile, Tigris, and Euphrates—the main "highways" of Egypt and Iraq—saw a great deal of river traffic.

Overland journeys were made by caravan, the merchandise loaded onto the backs of donkeys or, when crossing deserts, camels. Camel caravans traveled to and from China and India in the east, the shore of the Strait of Gibraltar in the west, and sub-Saharan Africa in the south. Along their route, they rested at caravanserais, large inns with food and shelter for animals as well as people. In cities, caravanserais that had storage space for goods were often known as *funduq*s. A *funduq* could also be a warehouse, headquarters, and social center for a group of foreign merchants. In the middle of the twelfth century, the geographer al-Idrisi reported that there were more than nine hundred *funduq*s in the Andalusian port city of Almería alone.

HOME SWEET HOME

In most of medieval Europe, people in the crafts and trades normally had their shops on the ground floor of their homes, the sales area opening out onto the street. This was not the case in Muslim cities, where home and business were kept completely separate, with residential neighborhoods away from the commercial districts. In Islamic culture, the home was a very private place. Whether it was a mansion or an apartment building, the wall facing the street would be plain, with any windows placed too high to see into. In fact, from the outside it could be nearly impossible to tell if you were walking by the home of a rich person or a poor one, especially since Muslims were discouraged from building showy houses. (One of Muhammad's sayings was, "Verily the most unprofitable thing that eats up the wealth of a believer is building.") Even if you looked through the entry gate and down the path inside, you would just see another blank wall.

But if you were a family member or invited guest and went on in through the gate, you would find that this path turned a corner and

The outside of an Andalusian house, still standing near the Great Mosque of Córdoba

led you to a courtyard. The courtyard might have trees and other plants, growing in the ground or in pots, and a fountain in the middle. Some courtyards had tiled floors; some had arbors overhead that provided shade but still allowed airflow. In any case, the courtyard was where many family activities took place, and it allowed light and air into the rooms surrounding it. These would include bedrooms, reception rooms, women's quarters, storerooms, and perhaps a kitchen—although cooking was frequently done in the courtyard or on the roof, which was generally flat.

The wealthier a family was, the more rooms they would have, often arranged around several courtyards. In some places houses had only one floor,

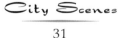

but in others they might have two or more. Al-Muqaddasi reported that in Fustat there were many apartment buildings of four or five stories, each housing as many as two hundred people. Both courtyard houses and apartment buildings used some ingenious methods of ventilation and cooling, while at the same time protecting the residents' privacy. Windows and balconies could be shielded by latticework or grills. Many buildings had *malqaf*s, or wind catchers. A *malqaf* was a shaft with an opening that projected above the roof and was positioned to catch the prevailing winds. For additional cooling, the air that came down the *malqaf* might be directed to flow over a pool or a piece of wet fabric stretched on a screen.

Furniture in the medieval Muslim world was quite different from what we are used to in the West today. Only people who were very wealthy or important had chairs or bed frames that were raised up on legs, which were symbols of high status. It was much more common for people to sit on pillows, rugs, or low sofas, and to sleep on mattresses or rugs on the ground. The very poor might only have a mat or just the bare floor to sleep on. Tables (for those who could afford them) were low to the ground, too.

Urban homes—especially apartment buildings—were often poorly equipped for cooking and baking. People who didn't have an oven had to take their bread dough to a public oven to bake it, or they might buy bread at a bakery. In the markets there were also restaurants and stalls that sold prepared food. One source estimates that Cairo had nearly 12,000 cooks selling marketplace meals.

Except for the wealthy, there was no form of indoor plumbing: people went to the bathroom in outhouses. Most city dwellers also lacked bathing facilities at home, although there was always water for washing face and hands. But for a real bath, a trip to the local public bathhouse was necessary. Some places had separate bath-

A bakery in Cairo, with loaves of fresh bread cooling on the counter. This illustration is from the 1880s, but the scene would have been much the same in the Middle Ages.

houses for men and women. In neighborhoods or towns where there was only one bathhouse, some days, or parts of the day, would be set aside for women, others for men. Either way, most Muslims went to the bathhouse at least once a week. Bathing was an enjoyable activity that people generally looked forward to—not only did they get clean, but they could also relax and socialize with their friends while they were doing so.

City Scenes

A Landlord's Worries

The essayist al-Jahiz told the story of a friend who was renting a house in Baghdad and invited two relatives to visit for a month. The landlord found out about the visitors and immediately raised the rent, explaining his reasons in the following letter:

There are several reasons that prompt me to adopt this attitude. . . . The first is that the cesspit fills up more quickly, and it costs a lot to have it emptied. Then, as the number of feet increases, there is more treading on the clay-surfaced flat roofs and the plastered

Above: Homes in the medieval Muslim world were furnished much like this nineteenth-century sitting room in southern Arabia (although water pipes, such as the one seen here, did not come into use until the 1500s or so).

floors of the bedrooms, and more wear and tear on the staircase: the clay flakes off, the plaster crumbles, and the steps get worn down. . . . When people are continually going in and out, opening and closing doors and drawing and shooting the bolt, the doors split and their fastenings get broken off. . . . Moreover the walls get ruined through people hammering in pegs and shelf-brackets.

When the number of members of the family, visitors, lodgers and guests goes up, there is ten times as much pouring of water and seepage from pitchers and jars as usual. Many a wall has been undermined, had its upper courses crumble and its foundations give way and threatened to collapse altogether, as the result of seepage from a pitcher or a jar, or because too much water was drawn from the well and the whole thing mishandled.

The requirements of bread, food, fuel and heating increase with the number of heads. Now fire is "no respecter of persons," and houses and their contents make ideal fuel for it. . . . [Tenants] choose to use the high rooms built on the flat roof as kitchens, even though there is ample space on the ground floor or in the courtyard—and this despite the danger to life and property that it causes. There is the further risk that in the event of fire the undamaged portions of the house are liable to be broken into by hooligans. . . .

When a tenant moves in, we will have swept and cleaned the house to make it look nice . . . ; when he moves out, he leaves filth and dilapidations that call for heavy expenditure. Moreover he never fails to take with him the beam used for wedging the door, the ladder, sundry building materials and the water-cooler. . . . It does not take long for houses to be in ruins. The tenants who live in them have the pleasure and benefit of them: it is they who wear them out and rob them of their freshness, and their ill-treatment that ages them and brings their end nigh.

THREE

A Man's World

Whoever in this world has half a loaf
enough for shelter and for sustenance
who is no man's servant and no man's master
let him be happy, for mortal bliss is his.

→ OMAR KHAYYAM, TWELFTH-CENTURY PERSIAN ASTRONOMER AND POET

I N MEDIEVAL ISLAMIC CULTURE, THE SEPARATION between business and home, public and private, also separated men from women to a great extent. Respectable women were expected to stay mostly in the privacy of the home, so the majority of people out in the markets and other public places—especially the workers—would be men. Men were expected to work hard, too, for it was their duty to provide for their wives, children, and other household members.

With this responsibility also came authority. The head of the family was the oldest male (usually the father but, if he was dead, the oldest son or brother), and he managed all of the family's property

Opposite: Traveling merchants arrive at a busy town. Behind them men and women argue and do business in the marketplace. This scene comes from a Baghdad manuscript from around 1237.

37

and business. Family bonds were at the heart of Muslim society, and people typically governed their actions by whether or not they would benefit the family as a whole. This was most important with regard to the immediate household, but it could also apply to a wider group of relatives who all descended from the same ancestor, even stretching back several generations.

MERCHANTS AND CRAFTSMEN

In business a large extended family could be a distinct advantage. Merchants often had agents in the other cities they traded with, who made financial arrangements, met incoming ships or caravans, and so on. It was very handy if those agents were cousins or nephews—the relationship would help ensure that everyone was working honestly and conscientiously.

Merchants did not always work with their families, though. Sometimes they formed partnerships with investors and fellow merchants; such arrangements were made on a venture-by-venture basis. Some merchants were also shipowners, while others had to hire ships if they wanted to send goods by water. In Cairo many of the ships that sailed the Nile, the Mediterranean Sea, and the Indian Ocean were owned by Jews. Cairo's Jewish community also included merchants who traded in person around the Mediterranean and with East Africa and India. One such merchant that we know of even lived in India for nine years.

The merchants who dealt with imports and exports and far-off cities on this scale were the elite of the business community. Much more numerous were ordinary shopkeepers. Some of these would sell the goods that the great merchants imported. Others, more humble, sold local products. The ninth-century Baghdad judge and writer Tanukhi described a shopkeeper of this type, a cloth dealer

Merchants from different parts of the medieval Muslim world make business deals and oversee the loading and unloading of ships at a bustling port.

who got into trouble because he had reportedly been complaining about the caliph. When brought for judgment, he said, "I am a tradesman, who understands nothing but thread and cotton, and how to talk to women and common people," and explained that he had actually been complaining about a market inspector who had not been doing his job. Luckily the caliph believed him, released him, and sent instead for the market inspector, who was "severely reprimanded" and "told to set it right, and to look after the travellers and tradesmen and bring them into order."

A Man's World

THE MEN IN CHARGE

In the medieval Muslim world a city (together with its surrounding countryside) was typically ruled by a governor appointed by the caliph or sultan. To help keep order, the governor had troops at his disposal; they were often Turkish slave-soldiers known as Mamluks. Lodged in barracks in the city's fortress, they functioned in many ways as a police force.

Each residential quarter had a headman, who may have been chosen from among the neighborhood's leading families simply by informal consensus rather than any kind of election. The governor's commands filtered down to the populace through these headmen.

A marketplace near one of the city gates of Jerusalem

In the marketplace, the governor's representative was the *muhtasib*, or market inspector, an important figure with wide responsibilities, as described by the vizier Nizam al-Mulk:

> In every city a [market inspector] must be appointed whose duty is to check scales and prices and to see that business is carried on in an orderly and upright manner. He must take particular care in regard to goods which are brought from outlying districts and sold in the bazaars to see that there is no fraud or dishonesty, that weights are kept true, and that moral and religious principles are observed.

Weights, used to balance scales, were especially important because most items were sold by weight, and it would be all too easy for a shopkeeper to cheat customers by weighing things out inaccurately. The *muhtasib* had the authority to punish dishonest merchants as he saw fit—for example, as happened in Córdoba, by having the offender led through the marketplace by a herald announcing, "This is . . . a thief and a criminal, who, by his cheating, consumes the wealth of Muslims. Recognize him so you may avoid him."

Many shops in the marketplace belonged to craftsmen who both produced and sold their goods there. During most of the medieval period, craftworkers in medieval Muslim cities seem to have been very loosely organized. Those in the same craft or trade often had family connections, usually shared the same street or section of the marketplace, and sometimes formed partnerships with one another. Factors like these gave them common interests, and they might also band together for social reasons. In some cities, different craft groups competed with one another over which could give the best feasts.

In Isfahan, according to fourteenth-century traveler Ibn Batuta, "members of each craft appoint one of their own number as head man over them"—but he may have functioned mainly as a kind of social director for the group, rather than representing its interests to the government or acting in any official role. The government was involved with overseeing the crafts, though. The market inspector, or *muhtasib*, policed the marketplace and had the power to punish shopkeepers who cheated their customers and craftsmen whose goods weren't up to standard. To help him carry out these responsibilities, he could appoint an overseer, called an *arif*, for each craft or trade.

A surgeon performs a procedure to drain excess abdominal fluid from his wide-awake patient.

Although craftsmen were supervised and regulated, at least to some extent, doctors in many cities were not. Almost anyone, regardless of education or experience, could set up as a medical practitioner. The eleventh-century Cairo physician Ibn Ridwan declared, "The ignorant doctor is more harmful to the body than a current pestilence or thieves." He had good reason for this opinion, since he knew of one "physician" who tried to cure a paralyzed man by dripping milk on his head, another who would not treat patients without first consulting an astrolabe (an instrument that determined the sun's position in the sky), and still another who came to Ibn Ridwan for a potion to make his beard longer and grayer so that he would look older and therefore more worthy of respect. Still, there were plenty of well-educated, conscientious doctors like Ibn Ridwan. Moreover, some of the most learned men in the Islamic world had studied medicine and made at least part of their living as physicians.

MEN OF LEARNING

"Seek knowledge, even as far as China" was one of Muhammad's sayings. Although few Muslim scholars visited China, many did take the Prophet's advice to travel for knowledge, going from city to city of the Dar al-Islam, learning, teaching, and often serving in government offices along the way. For example, the philosopher al-Farabi (870–950) went from his birthplace in what is now Turkestan to Baghdad and then to Damascus. Avicenna (980–1037)—who mastered many fields of study and wrote a comprehensive medical encyclopedia—was born and first studied in Bukhara, then went to Isfahan and other Persian cities, working as a physician and even occasionally as vizier in various courts as he continued to expand his knowledge. Religious scholar al-Ghazali (1058–1111) left his home in Persia to study and teach in Baghdad, then traveled to Damascus and to a number of religious centers in Palestine and Arabia before returning to Persia. The list could go on and on.

Success in the Sciences

Many of the learned men in medieval Muslim cities were scientific pioneers. One was al-Kindi (died ca. 870), who worked in Baghdad under the patronage of the caliphs. He studied and wrote about subjects as diverse as music, medicine, astronomy, sword making, and Greek philosophy. He developed new methods of creating and breaking codes, devised a way to measure the strength of drugs, and invented a great number of perfumes. Moreover, he was largely responsible for popularizing the use of Indian numerals, which later passed from the Dar al-Islam into Europe. (In Spain many of his works were translated into Latin, and they then became widely studied in European universities.) Today we usually refer to Indian numerals as Arabic numerals, and modern science and technology would probably be impossible without them.

Another pioneer was Iraqi scientist and philosopher Ibn al-Haytham, sometimes referred to as Alhazen (965–1039), who worked in Cairo from the age of thirty till his death. Among other ideas and achievements, he was the first person to explain that the eye sees objects as a result of light rays bouncing off those objects and hitting the lens of the eye. He and another Muslim scientist, al-Biruni (973–1048), were the first to realize that light travels faster than sound. Both al-Haytham and al-Biruni advocated a scientific method based on observation and experimentation.

Al-Biruni was born in what is now Uzbekistan but spent most of his career in Persia and Afghanistan. His contributions to science were advanced and varied: he calculated the circumference of the earth (with almost complete accuracy), he believed that the earth rotated on its axis and quite possibly revolved around the sun, he invented or improved on scientific instruments such as the astrolabe, he formulated a theory of gravity, he theorized that India had once been covered by the ocean, he developed new ways of doing algebra (which had been invented by an earlier Muslim mathematician, al-Khwarizmi), and much more. In addition he traveled to India (in the retinue of Sultan Mahmud of Ghazni), where he learned Sanskrit and studied Indian religion, philosophy, science, and medicine.

While al-Biruni's writings helped spread Indian knowledge, other Muslim scholars had taken on the task of translating the philosophical and scientific writings of ancient Greece. In ninth-century Baghdad, three wealthy brothers known as the Banu Musa were among the most noted patrons of this work. As their thirteenth-century biographer wrote:

From a seventeenth-century Turkish manuscript, Avicenna demonstrates the medical benefits of bathing *(left)*, moderate wine drinking *(top)*, and music *(right)*. The musician is playing an oud, ancestor of the European lute and still a popular instrument in the Middle East.

Their noble ambition was to master the ancient sciences and the books of the classical scholars and they devoted themselves to this project. They sent agents to the Byzantine Empire to bring them books. They attracted translators from distant lands and far off places by offering generous rewards. They made known the wonders of science.

The Banu Musa not only provided housing for a group of gifted translators (which included Christians as well as Muslims) but also paid them salaries equal to the earnings of government administrators. The cost was worth it—the translations produced here and

The City

elsewhere in the medieval Muslim world preserved numerous ancient Greek works that otherwise would have been lost.

Law and Literature

While many educated men had wide-ranging interests, most kept their main focus on Muslim religious studies. These scholars were known as the *ulama*. They were learned in the Qur'an, hadiths—the records of Muhammad's sayings and actions—and Islamic law. They served as religious leaders, teachers, lawyers, and judges (but not necessarily all at the same time). Judges, called *qadi*s, were not allowed to

Men gather to discuss books and ideas in the public library of Basra, Iraq, a popular meeting place for scholars and writers. Behind them are numerous compartments filled with stacks of books.

make their own legal interpretations but only to apply the accepted laws in disputes over property, inheritance, divorce, and similar matters. Each city had a chief *qadi*, appointed by the ruler, who could then appoint additional judges to serve under him.

One of the most famous men to serve as a *qadi* was Ibn Rushd, commonly known as Averroës (pronounced ah-VAIR-oh-eez; 1126–1198). The son and grandson of Córdoban *qadi*s, he held that office in both Seville and Córdoba. He also spent time in Marrakech (in Morocco) as adviser and physician to the ruler there. He was said to be so devoted to learning that he spent every night of his life studying, except for his wedding night and the night of his father's death. His studies included not only law and medicine but also

From her balcony window, Princess Shirin watches the arrival of King Khusraw, come to her castle to pledge his love. Nizami's long romantic poem was a favorite subject for artists.

Greek philosophy. He wrote extensive commentaries on the works of Plato and Aristotle, which were valued both in the Muslim world and (after being translated into Latin) in Christian Europe.

Many learned men were also talented poets. Poetry held a high place in Islamic culture, which prized the skillful use of words. Even scientific works were often written in verse. So it was natural for educated men to express themselves in poetry. For example, the noted Persian astronomer and mathematician Omar Khayyam composed four-line verses whenever inspiration struck him; today his poems, collected together as the *Rubaiyat*, are far better known than his scientific work.

Poets often found support and an audience in the courts of caliphs, sultans, and city governors. One of the greatest Persian poets, however, worked without such patronage. Nizami lived in the city of Ganja (Ganca in today's Azerbaijan) and became famous for his long romantic poems. One of them tells of the great love between the fabled Persian king Khusraw and an Armenian princess named Shirin. Here is part of a scene in which the king questions a stonemason who is also in love with Shirin:

First, the king asked him, "Where are you from?"
He replied: "From the capital of the realm of love."

"And what trade do they follow there?"
"They buy grief and sell souls."

"But selling souls is not good work."
"But not unknown to lovers."

"Did you fall in love with all your heart?"
"You speak of heart. I speak of soul."

Women at Home and Work

The ability of women is not known, because they are . . .
placed at the service of their husbands.

➤ AVERROËS, TWELFTH-CENTURY ANDALUSIAN JUDGE, DOCTOR, AND PHILOSOPHER

IT CAN BE A CHALLENGE TO LEARN MUCH ABOUT the lives of medieval Muslim women. There are numerous short biographies of notable women, especially from the fourteenth and fifteenth centuries, but generally only hints and scattered evidence for the everyday lives of average women. Almost all the authors of the period were men, and it was considered improper for them to write about women's private lives. The few works we have by women are mostly poems by high-ranking ladies associated with the courts of various rulers. However, one fifteenth-century Turkish poet, Mihri Hatun (Lady Mihri),

Opposite: Although this painting was made in the nineteenth century, the woman is spinning thread exactly as her ancestors did in ancient and medieval times, with distaff and drop spindle.

penned a verse that no doubt expressed the feelings of a great many women in all walks of life:

> Woman, they say, is deficient in sense
> so they ought to pardon her every word.
> But one female who knows what to do
> is better than a thousand males who don't.

HOME AND FAMILY

Almost all medieval Muslim women married. While Islamic law allowed a man to have as many as four wives (so long as he could provide equally for all of them), the ideal was really for a lifelong marriage between one man and one woman. However, divorce was permitted and not unusual. Both women and men had the right to ask for divorce (although it was harder for a woman to get one), and it was common for both to remarry afterward. Widows also usually remarried—some several times, since a woman's first marriage was usually made during her early teens to an older (sometimes much older) man.

A wife was expected to be completely devoted to her husband and their children. The husband was the undisputed head of the household. If the wife disrespected his authority, he was allowed to slap her—but never hard enough to cause any injury, and only as a last resort. On the whole, men were exhorted to treat their wives with patience and kindness. And if a husband broke Islamic law, violated the terms of the marriage contract, or misused his wife's dowry (his wedding gift to her), she had the right to appeal for justice to a *qadi*, who would almost certainly make the husband obey the law.

An important part of a husband's duty was to protect his wife and children from possible harm by strangers, particularly men from out-

The harem of an old house in Cairo has windows fitted with wooden lattices, or screens. Such lattices came into use during the medieval period to allow in light and air while protecting privacy. This scene was painted around 1875 by British artist Frank Dillon.

side the family. This was the reason for the harem, which was simply the private part of the home. Only for the family, it was where women and children stayed when men they weren't related to were visiting. In a wealthy household the harem could be a whole suite of rooms; in a more modest one it would be a single room. Even if a family lived in a one-room house or apartment, there would still be a corner that could be curtained or screened off as a protected place.

Only the wealthy, however, could afford to have women live in complete seclusion, seeing no one but family and female friends. In the lower classes, women often had to earn an income and rarely had servants to run errands for them outside the house. When a

Styles of veiling have varied from place to place and time to time throughout the Muslim world. These Moroccan women hold their robes closed so that nothing can be seen but their eyes.

woman had to go to a public place, such as the market, she was expected to separate herself from men who were not related to her. She did this by dressing in a modest way that included covering her hair and veiling her face. This style of dress gave her a kind of portable seclusion, designed to protect her even when she had to speak to or do business with strangers. Customs did vary, though, among different places and ethnic groups. For instance, the fourteenth-century Moroccan traveler Ibn Batuta wrote this about the Turks who had settled in Anatolia:

A remarkable thing which I saw in this country was the respect shown to women by the Turks, for they hold a more dignified position than the men. . . . I saw also the wives of the merchants and common [men]. [Their faces are] visible for the Turkish women do not veil themselves. Sometimes a woman will be accompanied by her husband and anyone seeing him would take him for one of her servants.

It is hard now to know just what Ibn Batuta meant about Turkish women's "more dignified position." But it is clear that many (if not most) people felt that women's role in the home and family was an extremely worthy one. The Iraqi essayist al-Jahiz even stated the opinion that "women are superior to men in certain respects: it is they that are asked in marriage, desired, loved and courted, and they that inspire self-sacrifice and require protection." Whether or not these things made women superior, it seems certain that women's contributions to the family were generally valued and respected.

WOMEN'S WORK

Women's work was not only essential to a family's well-being, but could inspire love and admiration, as in this glowing description a tenth-century merchant wrote about his wife:

> If you had seen her, even once, when she toils, with her apron around her. . . how she rushes and runs in every corner, everywhere . . . how she turns and bends, flies from the oven to the pot and back again immediately . . . how she fans the fire and how she prepares the spices—crushes and powders them— while her pretty face, blackened by smoke which leaves its mark on her smooth cheeks . . . the sight would enchant you.

Cooking was one of the tasks that took up a lot of a woman's day. Food preparation could be a long, laborious process. For example, grain had to be ground into flour before a woman could even start making bread. Grinding grain was such a particularly tiring and tedious job that the marriage contracts of some prosperous city women specified they would not be expected to do it. The chore would be passed on to a servant instead.

A wealthy woman might have many servants to help her take care of the household, but this was not the case with most women. They were personally responsible for all the cooking, cleaning, and childcare. They might also make some or all of the family's clothes,

A Persian woman uses a spinning wheel to pull the fibers from silk-worm cocoons and wind them into silk thread.

and this could involve not only sewing but—before sewing could even start—carding or combing the cotton, linen, or silk fibers; spinning them into thread; and then weaving the thread into cloth. Many women also made their own dyes to color the thread or cloth, and they often decorated finished garments with embroidery.

Cloth-making skills not only allowed women to clothe their families but also offered them the opportunity to earn income. Moreover, women could do this work at home; spinning was especially easy to fit in here and there amid the day's other tasks. In addition to making thread, fabric, and clothing, women could weave rugs and wall hangings. Whatever textiles they produced, though, would usually have to be taken to the market and sold on their behalf by middlemen.

Some women were employed in spinning and weaving workshops, which might be owned by well-to-do women. For example, in Cairo a woman called Umm Hani (1376–1466) used her inheritance to buy a "great workshop, famous for its enormous size and many spinning wheels." Her biographer went on to tell how "one of the descendants of the original owner challenged the legality of the sale in court, but . . . [the judge] ruled that the sale was legal, and confirmed her ownership of the workshop." In addition to being a successful businesswoman, Umm Hani, like a number of other women of her time, was also well known as a religious teacher.

Another women's profession was that of midwife. Midwives, even though they worked outside their own homes, were highly respected for their knowledge and abilities in helping women give birth. Most women who worked in public, though, generally belonged to the lower classes. Many of these working women—entertainers and hairdressers, for example—were not so well thought of, even though their jobs required special talents or skills. Less skilled women could work as bathhouse attendants, or as what we would call undertakers, washing the dead and preparing them for burial. Funerals also provided jobs for professional mourners, women hired to publicly (and loudly) lament the dead.

Scholars are not sure how much women worked in the production of arts and crafts other than textiles. Archaeological finds have added to what literary sources can tell us, though. For example, a piece of pottery from Fustat inscribed "work of Khadija" (a woman's name) shows that there was at least one female potter in that city, even though there is no mention of such craftswomen in the writings of the time. On the other hand, medieval Muslim authors did refer to a number of women calligraphers—and calligraphy was regarded as the highest of all art forms, since it was used to communicate the word of God as given in the Qur'an.

In Córdoba there were many women employed as copyists in the book market, producing Qur'ans. Some educated Córdoban

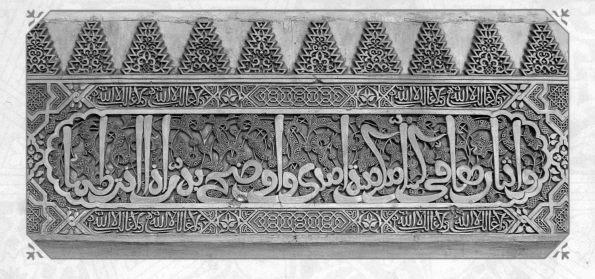

IMAGES IN ART

It is commonly thought that the Islamic tradition has always banned pictures of living things. The issue is not so simple, and was a matter of controversy in the Middle Ages (as it sometimes is today). People who were against such images might quote Muhammad's saying, "Those who make these pictures will be punished on the Day of Judgement by being told: Make alive what you have created." But other traditions about the Prophet could be called on to show that depictions of living beings were acceptable in at least some circumstances.

The main problem was the belief that artists who tried to produce lifelike images were guilty of denying God's role as sole creator and maker of things; it was as though these artists were trying to assume God's powers. A common solution to the problem, then, was to show people, animals, and plants in a flat, two-dimensional fashion, casting no shadows. This way, they would not look as if they were alive. In a religious setting, though, even this compromise was usually not acceptable because of the fear that images in this case might be turned into "idols" and worshipped. This is why most Muslims have objected to pictures of Muhammad and why mosques have traditionally been decorated mainly with abstract geometric designs, floral patterns, and stylized calligraphy of verses from the Qur'an.

Above: Plaster sculpted into calligraphy and geometric designs on a wall of the Alhambra palace in Granada

An upper-class Persian woman takes time out from a picnic to write—perhaps the beautiful outdoor setting has inspired a poem.

women also worked as physicians, lawyers, teachers, and librarians. In the tenth century the caliph's head librarian was a woman, Labna, and her deputy was a woman named Fatima. Knowledgeable, resourceful, and trustworthy, Fatima traveled widely in search of books to buy for the caliph's library. She visited not only Cairo, Damascus, Baghdad, Bukhara, and other Muslim cities but also Constantinople, the Byzantine capital. Muhammad's exhortation to seek knowledge, even in far places, was not just for men.

Women at Home and Work

A Coptic (Egyptian Christian) mother and child. Except for religion, medieval Copts adopted most aspects of Muslim culture.

FIVE

Growing Up in the City

*Prevention of the child from playing games and constant insistence on learning deadens
his heart, blunts his sharpness of wit and burdens his life.*
→→ AL-GHAZALI, ELEVENTH-CENTURY PERSIAN SCHOLAR AND MYSTIC

PEOPLE IN THE MEDIEVAL MUSLIM WORLD
thought of childhood as having four stages. The first was
from birth to teething. Second came the period from
teething to the "age of discernment"—that is, the age when children
could tell right from wrong. A child was thought to acquire this
moral sense at around seven years old. The next stage lasted till
about the age of fourteen, and the final one was the transition into
puberty and adulthood.

A large number of children did not make it through all these
stages. Death rates for the young, and especially for infants, were
high. The fifteenth-century writer Sakhawi and his wife, for example,
had at least ten children who died as babies. Sakhawi showed his love

and grief by including some of them in the biographical dictionary he wrote. His short biography of his daughter Juwayriyya concluded, "She died a few months after her birth . . . and was buried next to her brothers and sisters. May God compensate them with Paradise."

EARLY CHILDHOOD

Medieval Muslims believed it was every child's right to be breast-fed till the age of two. Normally mothers nursed their own babies; in general a wet nurse was hired only if the mother had died or was too ill or weak to breast-feed. During childhood there was no separation between males and females, so boys and girls alike spent most of their time with their mothers. They were closely looked after and generally treated with tenderness and even indulgence.

As children got past toddlerhood, they might start helping with some light, easy household tasks, especially in less well-off families. Parents would probably start teaching them the basics of Islam and, if they were literate, perhaps give them beginning lessons in reading and writing, too. But at this stage there was still plenty of playtime. Children had a variety of toys, including puppets, balls, and toy buildings and animals. Some very religious people, however, may not have permitted their daughters to have dolls because they were made in the human image. Most families allowed them, though, since tradition said that Muhammad's wife Aisha had played with dolls. Besides, people generally agreed that pretending to take care of a doll was good early practice for motherhood.

There were also many games, some enjoyed by adults as well as children. Board games included chess, backgammon, and mancala. Naturally there were ball games, pretend games, and other activities, too. Al-Jahiz wrote about children playing a game called *zadw* in the courtyard. This seems to have involved digging little holes and burying nuts or stones in them; the players evidently took turns guessing whether each hole contained an odd or even number of objects. Al-Jahiz also mentioned that children liked to scoot around on some sort of toy whose Arabic name has been translated as both "go-cart" and "wooden sled."

In some urban families, children had pets to play with. Cats were probably more common in the household than dogs. For one thing, cats made themselves very useful by killing rodents and other pests. Their habit of frequently washing themselves also made them appealing, since cleanliness was important to Muslims for both religious and practical reasons. Dogs seem to have been another matter; one of Muhammad's sayings was, "An angel will not enter a house in which there is a dog or a painting." The Prophet was said to have been very fond of cats, though. A story told how once while he was meditating, a cat curled up to sleep inside one of the wide sleeves of his robe. When his meditation was finished, he cut off the sleeve rather than disturb the sleeping cat.

A weaver teaches his sons the skills they will need to follow in his footsteps.

EDUCATION

Children began their serious education or training for their adult roles around the age of seven, and they could generally expect to follow in their parents' footsteps. Mothers taught their daughters how to cook, keep house, spin, weave, and sew. Fathers taught their craft or trade to their sons. Craft knowledge was

commonly passed down through multiple generations of an extended family, which might develop a near monopoly on the production of certain goods. For example, by 1300 the Abu Tahir clan had been the main makers of lusterware (a type of pottery) in the Persian city of Kashan for four generations. A boy could also get training by apprenticing with a master craftsman from outside his family, but apprenticeship in the medieval Muslim world does not seem to have been as formal as in Europe at the same period.

With regard to trades and professions, the Persian poet Saadi Shirazi recorded this advice that a wise teacher gave his students:

The city of Kashan was so famous for producing beautiful ceramic tiles—like this one featuring a charming rabbit, made in 1267—that *kashani* became the Persian word for "tile."

O darlings of your fathers, learn a trade because property and riches of the world are not to be relied upon; also silver and gold are an occasion of danger because either a thief may steal them at once or the owner spend them gradually; but a profession is a living fountain and permanent wealth; and although a professional man may lose riches, it does not matter because a profession is itself wealth and wherever he goes he will enjoy respect and sit in high places, whereas he who has no trade will glean crumbs and see hardships.

Upper-class families did follow such advice to a large extent, and boys received an education that would allow them to become merchants and businessmen, government officials, physicians, lawyers, or religious teachers. They could often receive at least part of their training at home from their fathers or other family members. At some point, though, they would probably go to school.

The core of early education was study of the Qur'an and Arabic, the language of the Qur'an. Students not only learned to read and write—practicing with pen and ink on a washable wooden tablet—but also memorized the Qur'an bit by bit. As students advanced, they would also study and memorize hadiths. Literacy and memory were both important in the medieval Muslim world, and it was felt that to really understand something, you had to know it by heart. As a twelfth-century Andalusian poet wrote:

This depiction of a student reading while his teacher looks on comes from an Arabic translation of an ancient Greek medical book. It was painted by a Syrian artist in 1229.

Knowledge in the heart is not knowledge in books;
So be not infatuated with fun and play.
Memorise, understand, and work hard to win it.
Great labour is needed; there is no other way.

In the earlier part of the medieval period, a boy would study first at home, then in the mosque, and then sometimes would go to live with and learn from a noted scholar. In the late 800s, rulers and wealthy people (including many women) began to fund the establishment of

schools called madrasas, meaning "places of study." Two of the many notable madrasa founders were the vizier Nizam al-Mulk (died in 1092) and Rabia Khatun (died in 1246), sister of Egypt and Syria's ruler Saladin. Madrasas might be associated with important mosques or be independent institutions. They often provided lodging for students and teachers as well as instructional space. The curriculum was focused on law and religious studies, although other subjects might also be taught.

Whether learning in a mosque, a scholar's home, or a madrasa, the diligent student listened to and carefully wrote down all the teacher's lectures. The teacher read out and commented on various texts and related the commentaries he had learned from his own teachers. When a student mastered a particular text and its commentaries, he received a certificate that gave him the authority to

The City

teach that text to others. Many students traveled far and wide, seeking out teachers who had mastered various texts. One such traveler was Ibn Asakir of Damascus. In 1126 he embarked on a fifteen-year journey that took him to Baghdad, Mecca and Medina, Isfahan, Nishapur, and on to Merv and other cities of Central Asia. During his travels he studied with nearly 1,400 teachers and learned hundreds—maybe thousands—of hadiths.

In scholarly families girls, too, often received an excellent education in the Qur'an and hadiths. Some learned not just at home but also in mosques and madrasas. Even where they weren't allowed to take formal classes, many times they could still attend study sessions and listen to public lectures. A number of women received certificates and went on to become respected teachers themselves. For example, at least eighty of the teachers that Ibn Asakir studied with were women. While there were always people who objected to women being educated, many others found it praiseworthy, recalling Muhammad's saying, "How splendid were the women of [Medina]; shame did not prevent them from becoming learned in the faith."

BECOMING AN ADULT

At puberty, boys and girls had to start observing the rules about separation between men and women, so this was when a girl started wearing the veil. She would probably get married around this time as well, if she wasn't already. Sometimes girls were married as young as nine or ten, although they probably were not expected to act as wives until after they reached puberty. Such youthful marriages were more like what we would think of as engagements. Boys tended to wait until they were in their twenties to marry, since they could not do so until they were able to financially support a family. They would spend the years between puberty and marriage furthering their education or establishing themselves in their craft or trade.

Marriages were nearly always arranged by the parents. The best match was generally felt to be between two cousins related on the father's side. This was because Islamic law was very specific about how much of a family's wealth each child should inherit, and a woman's portion went with her to her husband's family. If she married a paternal cousin, the property would still remain within the extended family. The next best thing to such a match was one that formed a connection with a wealthier or more powerful family.

Legally, marriage was a contract between the bride and groom. Often, however, they didn't meet until the actual wedding, and the marriage contract was negotiated by their families. One standard

The legendary Khusraw and Shirin in the happy ending of their story, alone together for the first time after their wedding

contractual matter was the amount of the dowry. In Islamic law this was property that the husband gave to his wife when they married. It remained hers throughout the marriage, to do with as she wished, and it was still hers if the marriage ended, whether in divorce or widowhood. Women (or their families) could also add personal provisions to the contract, as we have already seen with regard to grinding grain. Another term that a woman sometimes insisted on was that the husband not take any other wives so long as he was married to her.

The main purposes of Muslim marriage in the Middle Ages were to bring children into the world and to make alliances between families. Love and romance didn't enter into it. Because of the separation between the sexes, respectable young women had almost no opportunity to meet and fall in love with anyone. And since marriageable young women tended to be secluded within their families, romantic young men tended to fall in love with female slaves, who were not always subject to the same rules as free women. Nevertheless, many couples did end up finding love and contentment within marriage. The tenth-century merchant who was so entranced by his wife's beauty while cooking summed up his feelings on marriage this way: "Happiness is only granted to a man when it gives him a wife of the same mind—a life together with her in harmony and peace."

A pair of gazelles, from a manuscript produced around 1300. In medieval love poetry, a lover was often likened to a graceful gazelle.

Young Love

Ibn Hazm, a scholar and writer born in 994 in Córdoba, was the author of *The Ring of the Dove.* This famous book about love described unfulfilled yearning for an unattainable beloved in a way that would soon become popular in the romantic literature of Christian Europe as well. Here is a selection:

In my youth love drew me into a friendly relationship with a slave girl who had grown up in our house and was at the time sixteen years old. The beauty of her countenance, her intelligence, her chastity, purity, modesty and her pleasant nature were beyond compare. She would not consent to flirtation, refusing to sully her honor. Her friendliness was exceptional, yet she was always most careful to keep her face hidden by the veil. . . .

This girl had won my heart, and I fell passionately and helplessly in love with her. For some two years, I tried with all my energies to gain a hearing from her, and for once to pry from her lips words other than those [that] pass between people in public conversation. However, I had absolutely no success whatsoever.

Now I remember that one day a social gathering was held in our home. . . . [The guests] remained in the house for part of the day, and then there was a move to a belvedere [gazebo] near our house, perched above the garden. There were huge, open windows in the wall niches of the belvedere, which overlooked the whole of Córdoba. . . . I remember the joy I experienced at the proximity of the girl, and with the hope of lingering a while at her side, I advanced towards the window where she was standing. But no sooner did she become aware of my presence, than she left this window and at a sedate pace moved on to another one. . . . After this, they all went down to the garden, and now the older women and the elegant ladies of our circle requested the girl's mistress to permit her to sing us something. The girl took up her lute. . . . Then she began to sing. . . .

Upon my life! It was as if the plectron was plucking at my heart, and not the strings. I have never forgotten that day, and I shall not forget it until the day I depart this life. I never found another opportunity for seeing and listening to her.

SIX

Rest and Recreation

As night fell . . . in the neighborhood, the strains of lutes, drums and harps intermingled with singing would sound all around me . . . owing to the widespread habit of the people of this region in spending the nights singing and playing music.

↦ AHMAD AL-YAMANI, ELEVENTH-CENTURY ARABIAN TRAVELER

CITY PEOPLE WORKED HARD, BUT THEY FOUND many ways to relax. There were the pleasures of gossip with friends in the marketplace or the bathhouse. The marketplace also offered entertainment by jugglers and other performers, along with the always-interesting activity of people watching. Then there was quiet time with the family—sharing a meal, discussing the day's events, enjoying the coolness of evening in the courtyard. Every so often there was a holiday to celebrate, such as the great feast that ended Ramadan, the month in which adult Muslims fasted during the daylight hours. Two old Persian

Opposite: An enthusiastic reader, whose imagination seems to bring to life the people, animals, and fantastic creatures in his book

71

A group of men enjoy a pleasant time reading and playing games in a garden.

holidays also became popular in many cities: Nayruz at the spring equinox and Mihrjan at the autumn equinox. Both were occasions for giving gifts to friends and family members, especially children, who often received small pottery models of buildings and animals.

FESTIVE GATHERINGS

Family events provided city people with welcome opportunities for celebration. Seven days after the birth of a child, the family had a public feast, during which the child received its name. Even more festivity surrounded a boy's circumcision, usually at age seven or ten, or at the beginning of puberty. Medieval Muslims regarded this as an essential rite of purification, and undergoing it was an important stage in a boy's life.

Before the circumcision musicians led the boy, riding a horse, on a parade through the neighborhood, accompanied by his family and friends. Afterward, while he was recovering, his parents often threw a big party, with feasting and entertainment. A family that couldn't afford all this would still try to make the day as special as possible. One way to save money was to join up with a wedding procession, taking advantage of its music and merriment. As for wedding celebrations, they could go on for days and were as elaborate as the families could afford.

Even when there was no special occasion, well-to-do people enjoyed giving and attending dinner parties, which featured witty conversation as well as delectable food. Sometimes the food was served in bowls decorated with elaborate or highly stylized calligraphy. Once a bowl was empty, the guests would enjoy deciphering and discussing the writing, which was usually a wise or inspirational saying. For example, the following proverbs each decorated earthenware bowls made in tenth-century Persia:

The calligraphy on this Persian bowl says, "He who speaks, his speech is silver, but silence is a ruby."

> Planning before work protects you from regret; patience is the key to comfort.
> Knowledge is an ornament for youth and intelligence is a crown of gold.
> Generosity is the disposition of the dwellers of Paradise.

Banquets and parties often featured professional entertainment by musicians, singers, and sometimes male or female dancers. Unfortunately we have few descriptions of dance in the medieval Muslim world. The following short poem, however, gives us one brief but vivid image:

> The fire—a laughing dancer with whirling sleeves.
> She laughs at the wood, whose blackness
> Her dancing transforms to gold.

Unless all the guests at a party were female or family members, respectable women did not attend. On some occasions, though, they might be able to sit behind a screen, safely concealed from the male guests, and at least listen to the music and other entertainments. Otherwise the only women at most parties were the entertainers themselves, and perhaps servants. A traveler named Ahmad al-Yamani wrote about a men's musical gathering he happened upon while on a visit to the Andalusian city of Málaga in 1016:

> One night, as I lay awake . . . mysterious, low, delightful music could be heard . . . [and] a woman began to sing in a voice that was fresher than the flowers after rain. . . . I opened the door and followed the voice, which sounded near. From an aisle of my house, I discovered a spacious dwelling with a garden at the center of it. A gathering of some twenty men was assembled here, seated in rows, with drinks and fruit in their hands. By them stood slave-girls with lutes, tambourines, flutes and other instruments, but none of them were playing. The slave-girl, whom I had heard, sat some way apart with the lute in her lap. All present were gazing at her, as she sang and played.

LITERARY PASTIMES

Some gatherings included poetry readings, and poetry was enjoyed in other circumstances, too. People sometimes played a game in which one person improvised a line or two of verse, and their companion was supposed to improvise lines to finish the poem. Apparently people in all walks of life enjoyed this pastime. For example, there is a story about al-Mutamid, the ruler of Seville, strolling along a riverbank with his vizier. Al-Mutamid threw out this line: "The wind scuffs the river and makes it chain mail." The vizier couldn't think of anything that would rhyme, but a slave girl driving a mule nearby overheard and spoke up: "Chain mail for fighting could water avail." Not only did she supply the line needed to finish the verse, but she captured al-Mutamid's attention and his heart; they were later married.

Because of the importance of the Qur'an as the revealed and *written* word of God, a relatively large percentage of medieval Muslims were literate, especially in cities. Religious and philosophical studies were both a duty and a pleasure for many. Purely recreational reading was popular, too. Of course there was poetry of all kinds, and we have read many samples already. There were also histories, biographies, descriptions of foreign lands, fables, and stories.

One collection of stories from the medieval Muslim world, *The Thousand and One Nights* (or *Arabian Nights*), is especially famous today,

One of the heroes of *The Thousand and One Nights* soars high above the land on a magic flying carpet.

even outside the lands where it originated. The collection contains tales of kings and princesses, jinn (genies) and other magical beings, romance and trickery, dreadful villains, wondrous cities, marvelous animals, and more. Among its heroes are Aladdin, Ali Baba, Sinbad, and the caliph Harun ar-Rashid. The stories came from Persia and India as well as Iraq and the Muslim lands around the eastern Mediterranean.

The Thousand and One Nights were mainly folktales, and most medieval city dwellers were probably more likely to hear them from a marketplace storyteller than to read them in a book. Copied out and bound entirely by hand, books were expensive to buy. Still, they were more available, to more people, than they were in Christian Europe at this period. Besides the book-sellers in the marketplace, there were many types of private and public libraries, founded by rulers, attached to mosques, or run by professional scribes. Bookshops and libraries were also important social centers for educated people. One writer described the public library in Basra as "the haunt of the literary, and the rendezvous of all, whether residents or travellers."

Some libraries contained only religious and scholarly works and some let you read the books only in the library, but others let you check

Animal fables were enjoyed by people of all ages and social ranks. In this illustration from a popular collection of stories, a lioness gathers cheetahs, rabbits, and other animals for a conference.

The City

out books for a fee. No matter how people got access to books, they treasured them—and probably no one expressed the value of books, and his love for them, better than al-Jahiz:

> A book is a receptacle filled with knowledge, a container crammed with good sense, a vessel full of jesting and earnestness. It . . . will amuse you with anecdotes, inform you on all manner of astonishing marvels, entertain you with jokes or move you with homilies, just as you please. . . . I know no companion more prompt to hand, more rewarding, more helpful or less burdensome. . . . A book, if you consider, is something that prolongs your pleasure, sharpens your mind, loosens your tongue, lends agility to your fingers and emphasis to your words, gladdens your mind, fills your heart and enables you to win the respect of the lowly and the friendship of the mighty.

A woman cards wool to eke out a living for herself and her child.

SEVEN

Urban Hardships

At times of distress, strengthen your heart
Even if you stand at death's door.
The lamp has light before it is extinguished.
Wounded lions still know how to roar.

→→ SAMUEL HA-NAGID, ELEVENTH-CENTURY JEWISH ANDALUSIAN VIZIER,
GENERAL, AND POET

LIKE ALL CITIES THROUGH HISTORY, THE CITIES of the medieval Muslim world had their share of problems. People flocked to urban centers looking for opportunity—but not everyone found it. Cities always had a population of jobless and homeless people. Some got by as beggars, others as thieves; some didn't get by at all and died in the streets or, if they were lucky, in a charity hospital. Others eked out a living doing manual labor and odd jobs, making their homes in tiny apartments with few comforts. As splendid and highly cultured as cities such as Cairo and Damascus were, they had little to offer the very poor except the generosity of those who were better off.

Luckily, many found it, as Ibn Batuta reported of Mecca, whose citizens were

> distinguished by many excellent and noble activities and qualities, by their beneficence to the humble and weak, and by their kindness to strangers. When any of them makes a feast, he begins by giving food to the religious devotees who are poor and without resources, inviting them first with kindness and delicacy.

EVERYDAY ANNOYANCES

Rich or poor, city residents all had to cope with some of the same difficulties. With so many people concentrated in one place, noise was always an issue. So was crowding, especially since the streets in most urban areas were very narrow—even in the marketplace, there might be only room enough for two pack animals to pass each other. (There was rarely wheeled traffic to worry about—since carts, wagons, and so on were not used in most Islamic countries during this period.)

Where there were donkeys, horses, and camels, there was also manure. Since indoor plumbing was rare, human waste could be a problem, too; there were open sewers, and it was not unusual for men to simply step into an alley to go to the bathroom. Waste and garbage, which was sometimes just swept out into the street, could create a very smelly environment. Odorous industries made some parts of town even worse—for example, the areas where butchers and tanners worked.

Air quality was affected not only by noxious smells but also by smoke from cooking fires, pottery kilns, and the furnaces that heated water in the bathhouses. No wonder the physician-philosopher Moses Maimonides, a leading figure in the Jewish communities of

A camel struggles against its tether, no doubt making a great deal of noise in the process.

Córdoba and Cairo, declared, "Comparing the air of cities to the air of deserts and forests is like comparing thick and turbid waters to pure and light waters. . . . And if you . . . cannot emigrate from the city, at least try to live on the outskirts."

Water could be a problem, too. Muslim engineers were highly skilled at building aqueducts, reservoirs, and other systems to provide cities with reliable water supplies. But they generally couldn't do much to guarantee the water was clean and safe to drink—especially when its source was a much-used river. For example, al-Muqaddasi described the water in Basra (located where the Tigris and Euphrates join shortly before flowing into the Persian Gulf) as "one-third seawater, one third tidewater, and one third sewage. This is because at ebb tide the canal banks are laid bare and people relieve their bowels there: then the tide coming in carries the excrement with it."

Urban Hardships

Water sellers were a common sight in city streets.

Consequently, the citizens of Basra had their drinking water shipped to them from farther upstream.

In Cairo and other places, one of a woman's (or her servants') daily chores was to purify drinking water. This could require several stages of treatment, including heating, skimming out pollutants, and pouring the water through various substances. The physician Ibn Ridwan had several recipes for water-filtration mixes. One included clay, chalk, and vinegar, and another combined thyme, dill, almonds, and apricot pits. After purification, drinking water was stored in stone or earthenware jars, which usually had filters made of pottery in their necks to keep out insects.

Insects were a problem for everyone. Even upper-class people were bothered by fleas, as the Abbasid poet-prince Ibn al-Mutazz wrote:

I passed the whole night not closing my eyes.
The fleas like scattered fluff,
sated and half-sated bloodsuckers,
biting through hollow hairs,
plaguing the spirit if not destroying it,
boring into the skin, even through the cloak.

Other insect pests included lice, mosquitoes, cockroaches, and flies. Al-Jahiz told this story about a *qadi* in Basra who was famous for sitting perfectly still in court all day—until one day when a fly landed on his nose:

> It lingered there awhile, and then moved to the corner of his eye. He left it alone and endured its biting. . . . However, since the fly was . . . causing him acute pain and moving towards a spot where it was beyond bearing, he blinked his eyelid. The fly did not go away. . . . The *qadi*'s endurance was weakening and his irritation growing: he blinked harder and more rapidly. The fly . . . became so persistent that our *qadi*, his patience completely at an end, was reduced to driving it away with his hand. . . . The fly went away until he dropped his hand, then returned to the charge and compelled him to protect his face with the hem of his sleeve, not once but several times. . . . "God forgive me! . . . Now I know I am but a weakling, seeing that God's most feeble creature has vanquished and confounded me."

DANGEROUS TIMES

People generally learned to put up with insects, smells, noise, and crowds. Such things were simply part of the fabric of everyday life, which, after all, no one could expect to be perfect. Sometimes, though, conditions in a city got bad enough to lead to unrest and rioting. In particular, an unpopular ruler could provoke citizens into violent action. In 862, for instance, Turkish troops in Samarra staged a military coup and made their own candidate caliph instead of the man most people recognized as the rightful heir. On the day the new caliph was receiving his officials' oaths of allegiance, fifty horsemen serving the governor of Baghdad attacked the Turkish soldiers stationed along Samarra's main route. Fighting in the streets followed, spilling over into the caliph's public audience hall. The common people got involved, too.

Urban Hardships

One witness told how "sellers of barley-juice and dried fruits, bath attendants, water carriers and rabble from the markets"—along with escaped prisoners—looted the audience hall and nearby armory, then attacked and disarmed all the Turkish soldiers they could find.

There was more violence the next year and it soon spread to Baghdad. By 865 there was all-out civil war, and Baghdad came under siege. It was not the first time (and, sadly, would not be the last). In 812–813 Baghdad had been besieged during the Great Abbasid Civil War. The suffering of the people was terrible. One poet lamented:

> Here are people who have been overcome and burned by flames
> There a woman mourns a drowned man
> Here a beautiful, dark-eyed woman
> In a perfumed shift
> Flees from the fire into the looting
> While her father flees from the looting to the fire.
> Call on someone to take pity, but there is none to take pity. . . .

Similar scenes played out throughout the medieval Muslim world—when Crusaders attacked Jerusalem, when North African invaders and Christian kings conquered the cities of al-Andalus, when the Mongols swept through the whole eastern portion of the Dar al-Islam, in 1258 destroying Baghdad and the caliphate itself.

Those who survived the disasters of war were never the same—nor were their cities. The poet Ibn Hazm fled his native Córdoba when it was sacked by North African troops in 1013. Many years later he returned to the scene:

> I stood upon the ruins of our house, its traces wiped out, its signs erased, its familiar spots vanished. Decay had turned its

cultivated bloom to sterile waste. . . . Those elegant apartments, the plaything of destruction, were wilder now than the gaping mouths of lions, announcing the end of the world, revealing the fate of its inhabitants. . . .

Yet the world did not end, and traces of the great urban centers of medieval Islam were not entirely wiped out. The people of those cities made incredible and lasting contributions in art, architecture, literature, mathematics, science, philosophy, and religious thought. Many of the cities themselves continue to exist and thrive. Moreover, the faith community that was established in the Muslim cities of the Middle Ages has only grown in the succeeding centuries. And in spite of the wars that have been waged both for and against Islam—in spite of the violence done in the names of various faiths—the Qur'an continues to remind believers of the interconnectedness of all people: "Whosoever kills an innocent human being, it shall be as if he has killed all humankind."

A battle between Muslim soldiers and Christian Crusaders in twelfth-century Syria. The two sides were not always at war, however—there were long periods during which Syrian Muslims and Crusaders who settled in the region lived together in neighborly peace.

Urban Hardships

Glossary

al-Andalus the part of the Iberian Peninsula (modern Spain and Portugal) ruled by Muslims; also called Andalusia

brocade silk fabric with raised designs woven into it; the designs were often made with gold or silver thread

Byzantine Empire the Greek-speaking, eastern half of the ancient Roman Empire, with its capital at Constantinople. Arabic speakers generally referred to it as Rum ("Rome").

caliph (Arabic *khalifa*) the political and spiritual leader of the Muslim community, ruling as Muhammad's successor and deputy

calligraphy literally, "beautiful writing." In the Muslim world calligraphy became a highly developed and esteemed art form, often using extremely stylized letters.

caravanserai (Persian *karvansarai*) an inn built around a large open courtyard where caravans could rest

dynasty a series of rulers, usually related by family ties

garrison an army base

hadith a traditional statement by or about Muhammad. Hadiths ("reports") were remembered and passed on by his family and followers and later gathered together into several authoritative collections.

Persia modern-day Iran

qadi a judge in an Islamic law court

Sasanian Empire a Persian empire that stretched from the Euphrates River to the borders of India. It lasted from around 226 to 642, when it fell to the Muslim Arabs.

sultan (literally "authority" or "power") the Arabic term for a monarch or king; it eventually became the most common title for a Muslim ruler

Syria during the medieval period often used as the common name for the eastern Mediterranean region, including the modern countries of

Jordan, Israel, Palestine, and Lebanon as well as Syria; called al-Sham in Arabic

Turks members of a variety of Turkish-speaking nomadic tribes from Central Asia. Eventually they would become the dominant people in Anatolia, which as a result is now known as Turkey.

umma the community of Muslims

vizier (Arabic *wazir*) a chief administrator appointed by the ruler and under his direct authority

For Further Reading

Barber, Nicola. *Everyday Life in the Ancient Arab and Islamic World.* North Mankato, MN: Smart Apple Media, 2006.

Colombo, Monica. *The Islamic World: From Its Origins to the 16th Century.* Translated by Pamela Swinglehurst. Austin, TX: Raintree Steck-Vaughn, 1994.

Doak, Robin. *Empire of the Islamic World.* New York: Facts on File, 2005.

Dunn, John. *The Spread of Islam.* San Diego: Lucent Books, 1996.

George, Linda S. *The Golden Age of Islam.* New York: Benchmark Books, 1998.

Nicolle, David. *Historical Atlas of the Islamic World.* New York: Checkmark Books, 2003.

Online Information

Abaza, Ismail. "Saladin (Salah al-Din Yusuf Ibn Ayyub) and His Cairo." http://www.touregypt.net/featurestories/saladin.htm

Bartel, Nick. *Medieval Islamic Cultures.* http://www.sfusd.k12.ca.us/schwww/sch618/Islam_New_Main.html

Foundation for Science Technology and Civilisation. *Muslim Heritage.*
  http://www.muslimheritage.com
Lunde, Paul. "Science: The Islamic Legacy."
  http://saudiaramcoworld.com/issue/198203/science-the.islamic.legacy.htm
Stone, Caroline. "The Muhtasib."
  http://www.saudiaramcoworld.com/issue/197705/the.muhtasib.htm
Unity Productions Foundation. *Cities of Light: The Rise and Fall of Islamic Spain.*
  http://www.islamicspain.tv/Arts-and-Science/The-Culture-of-Al-
  Andalus/index.html

Selected Bibliography

Bartel, Nick. *Islam: Women, Marriage, and Family.*
  http://www.sfusd.k12.ca.us/schwww/sch618/Women/Islam_Women,_
  Marriage_and_.html
Brett, Michael. *The Moors: Islam in the West.* London: Orbis Publishing, 1980.
Burckhardt, Titus. *Moorish Culture in Spain.* Translated by Alisa Jaffa. New
  York: McGraw-Hill, 1972.
Editors of Time-Life Books. *What Life Was Like in the Lands of the Prophet:
  Islamic World AD 570–1405.* Alexandria, VA: Time-Life Books, 1999.
Esposito, John L., ed. *The Oxford History of Islam.* New York: Oxford
  University Press, 1999.
Fletcher, Richard. *Moorish Spain.* New York: Henry Holt, 1992.
Hill, Fred James, and Nicholas Awde. *A History of the Islamic World.* New
  York: Hippocrene Books, 2003.
Irwin, Robert. *Islamic Art in Context: Art, Architecture, and the Literary World.*
  New York: Harry N. Abrams, 1997.
Irwin, Robert, ed. *Night and Horses and the Desert: An Anthology of Classical
  Arabic Literature.* Woodstock, NY: The Overlook Press, 1999.
Kennedy, Hugh. *When Baghdad Ruled the Muslim World: The Rise and Fall of*

Islam's Greatest Dynasty. Cambridge, MA: Da Capo Press, 2005.

Lewis, Bernard, trans. *Music of a Distant Drum: Classical Arabic, Persian, Turkish, and Hebrew Poems.* Princeton, NJ: Princeton University Press, 2001.

Lindsay, James E. *Daily Life in the Medieval Islamic World.* Westport, CT: Greenwood Press, 2005.

Lowney, Chris. *A Vanished World: Muslims, Christians, and Jews in Medieval Spain.* New York: Oxford University Press, 2005.

McNeill, William H., and Marilyn Robinson Waldman, eds. *The Islamic World* (Readings in World History, vol. 6). New York: Oxford University Press, 1973.

O'Callaghan, Joseph F. *A History of Medieval Spain.* Ithaca, NY: Cornell University Press, 1975.

Robinson, Francis, ed. *The Cambridge Illustrated History of the Islamic World.* Cambridge: Cambridge University Press, 1996.

Shabbas, Audrey, ed. *A Medieval Banquet in the Alhambra Palace.* Rev. ed. Berkeley, CA: AWAIR: Arab World and Islamic Resources and School Services, 1993.

Sources for Quotations

Chapter 1

p. 13 "These centers": O'Callaghan, *A History of Medieval Spain*, p. 356.

p. 14 "Whatever you may disagree": Robinson, *The Cambridge Illustrated History of the Islamic World*, p. 7.

p. 14 "a community": ibid., p. 6.

p. 15 "My heart": Lewis, *Music of a Distant Drum*, p. 186.

p. 16 "She is the paradise": Lindsay, *Daily Life in the Medieval Islamic World*, p. 93.

p. 17 "It is best to settle": Hill and Awde, *A History of the Islamic World*, p. 53.

p. 19 "This figure": Shabbas, *A Medieval Banquet in the Alhambra Palace*, pp. 14–15.

p. 19 "elevated with honors": Lowney, *A Vanished World*, p. 63.

p. 20 "It has superceded": Lindsay, *Daily Life in the Medieval Islamic World*, pp. 106–107.

p. 21 "manuscripts in all": Time-Life, *What Life Was Like in the Lands of the Prophet*, p. 101.

p. 21 "the mother of the world": ibid., p. 115.

Chapter 2

p. 23 "Córdoba is made": Shabbas, *A Medieval Banquet in the Alhambra Palace*, p. 14.

p. 24 "Al-Mutasim had architects": Irwin, *Islamic Art in Context*, p. 73.

p. 24 "City mosques": Robinson, *The Cambridge Illustrated History of the Islamic World*, p. 168.

p. 24 "The caliph al-Walid": Irwin, *Islamic Art in Context*, p. 72.

p. 26 "one of the foundations": Lindsay, *Daily Life in the Medieval Islamic World*, p. 114.

p. 28 "On the north side": ibid., p. 108.

p. 29 "From Damascus": ibid., p. 97.

p. 29 "From Jerusalem": ibid., pp. 96–97.

p. 29 "Merchants come": O'Callaghan, *A History of Medieval Spain*, pp. 156–157.

p. 31 "Verily the most": Irwin, *Islamic Art in Context*, p. 83.

p. 34 "There are several reasons": McNeill and Waldman, *The Islamic World*, pp. 127–129.

Chapter 3

p. 37 "Whoever in this world": Lewis, *Music of a Distant Drum*, p. 106.

p. 39 "I am a tradesman," "severely reprimanded," etc.: McNeill and Waldman, *The Islamic World*, p. 107.

p. 40 "In every city": Lindsay, *Daily Life in the Medieval Islamic World*, p. 114.

p. 40 "This is . . . a thief": O'Callaghan, *A History of Medieval Spain*, p. 156.

p. 41 "members of each": Irwin, *Islamic Art in Context*, p. 135.

p. 41 "The ignorant doctor": Time-Life, *What Life Was Like in the Lands of the Prophet*, p. 102.

p. 42 "Seek knowledge": Hill and Awde, *A History of the Islamic World*, p. 119.

p. 44 "Their noble ambition": Kennedy, *When Baghdad Ruled the Muslim World*, pp. 254–255.

p. 47 "First, the king asked": Lewis, *Music of a Distant Drum*, p. 117.

Chapter 4

p. 49 "The ability of women": Lowney, *A Vanished World*, p. 170.

p. 50 "Woman, they say": Lewis, *Music of a Distant Drum*, p. 151.

p. 52 "A remarkable thing": Bartel, *Islam: Women, Marriage, and Family*.

p. 53 "women are superior": McNeill and Waldman, *The Islamic World*, p. 131.

p. 53 "If you had seen": Bartel, *Islam: Women, Marriage, and Family*.

p. 55 "great workshop" and "one of the descendants": Robinson, *The Cambridge Illustrated History of the Islamic World*, p. 190.

p. 55 "work of Khadija": Irwin, *Islamic Art in Context*, p. 140.

p. 56 "Those who make": ibid., pp. 80–81.

Chapter 5

p. 59 "Prevention of the child": Lindsay, *Daily Life in the Medieval Islamic World*, p. 195.

p. 60 "She died": Robinson, *The Cambridge Illustrated History of the Islamic World*, p. 197.

p. 61 "An angel": Irwin, *Islamic Art in Context*, p. 80.

p. 62 "O darlings": *The Golestan of Saadi*, p. 154, PDF accessed from http://www.iranchamber.com/literature/saadi/saadi.php

p. 63 "Knowledge in the heart": Irwin, *Night and Horses and the Desert*, p. 354.

p. 65 "How splendid": Lindsay, *Daily Life in the Medieval Islamic World*, p. 196.

p. 67 "Happiness is only": Bartel, *Islam: Women, Marriage, and Family*.

p. 69 "In my youth": Burckhardt, *Moorish Culture in Spain*, pp. 95–96.

Chapter 6

p. 71 "As night fell": Burckhardt, *Moorish Culture in Spain*, p. 90.

p. 73 "Planning" and "Knowledge": Esposito, *The Oxford History of Islam*, p. 226.

p. 73 "Generosity": Irwin, *Islamic Art in Context*, p. 167.

p. 73 "The fire": Burckhardt, *Moorish Culture in Spain*, p. 91.

p. 74 "One night": ibid., p. 90.

p. 74 "The wind": Shabbas, *A Medieval Banquet in the Alhambra Palace*, p. 19.

p. 75 "Chain mail": ibid., p. 19.

p. 76 "the haunt": Irwin, *Night and Horses and the Desert*, p. 150.

p. 77 "A book": ibid., pp. 86–88.

Chapter 7

p. 79 "At times of distress": Fletcher, *Moorish Spain*, p. 96.

p. 80 "distinguished by many": Hill and Awde, *A History of the Islamic World*, p. 110.

p. 81 "Comparing the air": Lowney, *A Vanished World*, p. 155.

p. 81 "one-third seawater": Lindsay, *Daily Life in the Medieval Islamic World*, p. 102.

p. 82 "I passed": Lewis, *Music of a Distant Drum*, p. 60.

p. 83 "It lingered there": Irwin, *Night and Horses and the Desert*, pp. 90–91.

p. 84 "sellers of barley-juice": Kennedy, *When Baghdad Ruled the Muslim World*, pp. 273–274.

p. 84 "Here are people": ibid., p. 105.

p. 84 "I stood upon the ruins": Brett, *The Moors*, p. 66.

p. 85 "Whosoever kills": Qur'an 5:32, in Lowney, *A Vanished World*, p. 4.

Index

Index

Index

About the Author

KATHRYN HINDS grew up near Rochester, New York. She studied music and writing at Barnard College, and went on to do graduate work in comparative literature and medieval studies at the City University of New York. She has written more than thirty books for young people, including the books in the series LIFE IN ELIZABETHAN ENGLAND, LIFE IN ANCIENT EGYPT, LIFE IN THE ROMAN EMPIRE, LIFE IN THE RENAISSANCE, and LIFE IN THE MIDDLE AGES. Kathryn lives in the north Georgia mountains with her husband, their son, and an assortment of cats and dogs. In addition to writing, she is a teacher and performer of Middle Eastern dance and music, which she has been studying for twenty years. She is always learning more. Visit Kathryn online at http://www.kathrynhinds.com

About Our Consultant

DR. JOSEF W. (YOUSEF) MERI, Fellow and Special Scholar in Residence at the Royal Aal al-Bayt Institute for Islamic Thought in Amman, Jordan, has also been a visiting scholar at the American Research Centre in Egypt; the Hebrew University of Jerusalem; L'Institut Français d'Études Arabes in Damascus; the Near Eastern Studies Department at the University of California, Berkeley; and the Institute of Ismaili Studies, London. He earned his doctorate at Oxford University, specializing in medieval Islamic history and religion and in the history and culture of the Jews of the Near East. He is the author or co-author of numerous journal articles, encyclopedia entries, and books, including *The Cult of Saints Among Muslims and Jews in Medieval Syria* (Oxford: Oxford University Press, 2002), and he was general editor of *Medieval Islamic Civilization: An Encyclopedia* (New York and Oxford: Routledge, 2006).